THE BIGGEST

FASCINATING FACTS

David Armentrout

Rourke Press, Inc.
Beach, Florida 32964

PHOTO CREDITS
© Columbus Southern Power/Ohio Power: pgs. 12, 13; © Dick
Dietrich: Left Cover, pg. 4; © Bob Firth/Int'l Stock: pg. 17;
© 1994 Monterey Bay Aquarium, Photography by
Rob Lewine: pg. 8; © James P. Rowan: Right Cover, Title page,
pgs. 15, 18, 21; © Luba Vangelova: pg. 7;
© Suzanne A. Vlamis/Int'l Stock: pg. 10

Library of Congress Cataloging-in-Publication Data

Armentrout, David, 1962–
   The biggest / by David Armentrout.
     p. cm. — (Fascinating facts)
   ISBN 1-57103-126-X
   Summary: Brief presentations of facts about some of the biggest
things in the world, such as the blue whale and the Grand Canyon.
   1. Size perception—Juvenile literature. [1. Size.]
I. Title II. Series: Armentrout, David, 1962- Fascinating facts.
BF299.S5A76 1996
031.02—dc20

                       96–20862
                       CIP
                       AC

Printed in the USA

TABLE OF CONTENTS

CANYON

A canyon, or gorge, is a deep valley with steep rock walls on both sides. The biggest land gorge is the Grand Canyon in Arizona.

The Grand Canyon is 277 miles long and ten miles across. It is over a mile deep in some places.

Even the Grand Canyon seems small when compared to the largest underwater canyon: The Labrador Basin spans 2,150 miles under the Atlantic Ocean, off the Coast of Newfoundland.

The biggest land gorge in the world is the Grand Canyon

LIZARD

Monitor lizards come in all sizes. They range from eight inches to over ten feet. The largest of them all is the **Komodo dragon** (kuh MO do) (DRAG un), which may weigh 500 pounds.

Komodo dragons are **carnivorous** (kahr NIV ur us). This means they eat other animals. Using their sharp teeth and claws, the Komodo dragon feeds on animals the size of goats and deer.

An adult Komodo dragon is a fierce **predator** (PRED uh ter) and can be a danger to people.

A giant monitor lizard is a dangerous predator

AQUARIUM

An aquarium is a tank that holds **marine** (muh REEN) plants and animals. They come in all shapes and sizes. Pet fish, turtles, and even lizards are kept in home aquariums.

Hundreds of big public aquariums around the world give people a look at life in the sea. The largest aquarium in the world is in Orlando, Florida. It holds over 6 million gallons of water.

The Monterey Bay aquarium in California has the largest display of marine life. It contains more than 6,500 marine animals and plants.

The bubble allows people to get a closer look at aquarium exhibits

SEA ANIMAL

The blue whale is not only the largest living animal, but also the largest creature ever known. At birth, a blue whale is 23 feet long and weighs as much as a full-grown elephant. Blue whales may reach over 110 feet and 150 tons, or 300,000 pounds!

Hunting nearly caused **extinction** (ex STINGK shun), or loss, of the blue whale in the 1960's. The blue whale is now an **endangered species** (en DAYN jerd) (SPEE sheez), and hunting them is no longer allowed.

The largest creature on Earth is the blue whale

The biggest mobile land machine, "Big Muskie," weighs over 13,000 tons

The bucket of "Big Muskie," a coal digger, can hold a city bus

BEAR

Of the many kinds of bears, the biggest live on the Island of **Kodiak** (KO dee AK) in Alaska. Alaskan brown bears, or Kodiak bears, are the biggest carnivorous, or meat-eating, animals on land.

A full-grown Kodiak bear may weigh 1,700 pounds and stand ten feet tall. To get so big, these giant bears eat huge amounts of salmon that fill nearby streams every summer.

Bears usually avoid people, but it is worth noting that bears are short-tempered and can kill a person with the swipe of a paw.

14   *The Kodiak bear is native to Kodiak Island off the Coast of Alaska*

ICE SCULPTURE

Who doesn't like an ice sculpture? In many parts of the world people carve, or sculpt, ice. Some of them turn out works of art.

The world's largest ice form was built in January, 1992 for the Winter Carnival in Minnesota.

The 166-foot "ice palace" was made with 18,000 blocks of ice. The palace covered an area the size of a football field and contained more than 10 million pounds of ice.

The world's largest ice form was built for the 1992 Winter Carnival in Minnesota

REPTILE

One of the scariest animals in the world is the crocodile. Its huge mouth is rimmed with long, sharp teeth. This largest of all reptiles grows to 23 feet and may weigh more than a ton.

It's hard to imagine that such a fierce-looking animal should have to worry about survival. Due to overhunting for skins and food, though, some species of crocodiles are faced with extinction.

Crocodiles bask in the sun during the day, often with their mouths open

LAND ANIMAL

The largest living land animal is the elephant. Elephants live in the wild in parts of Africa and Southeast Asia. The biggest elephants grow to thirteen feet and weigh over 16,000 pounds.

The elephant's trunk is its most amazing feature. Elephants use their trunks to smell, pull down trees, pick up small objects, and suck up water to drink. Some elephants drink 50 gallons of water and eat almost 500 pounds of plants every day.

An elephant uses its trunk to suck up water before bringing the water to its mouth to drink

DIGGING MACHINE

Digging machines are used all over the world to help build roads and buildings and to dig minerals from the ground.

Big Muskie is the name of the biggest mobile land machine ever made. The Ohio Power Company used it to dig coal.

Big Muskie has a bucket at the end of a long boom, or arm, to pick up loads of earth. The bucket can dig twenty truck loads of dirt in a single scoop.

Glossary

carnivorous (kahr NIV ur us) — feeding on animals

endangered species (en DAYN jerd) (SPEE sheez) — a kind of animal in danger of no longer existing or living

extinction (ex STINGK shun) — no longer existing or living

Kodiak (KO dee AK) — an island off the coast of Alaska and the name given to the large brown bear that lives there

Komodo dragon (kuh MO do) (DRAG un)— the name given to the largest monitor lizard

marine (muh REEN) — of or relating to the sea

predator (PRED uh ter) — an animal that kills another animal for food

INDEX

031.02
A

Armentrout

031.02
A

Armentrout

The biggest

DATE DUE	BORROWER'S NAME	ROOM NUMBER

DEMCO